Social Media

How to Leverage The Power of Facebook
Advertising, Instagram, YouTube and SEO
For Promoting Your Personal Brand

Jason Miller

2019

Disclaimer

The content contained within this book may not be reproduced, duplicated or transmitted without direct written permission from the author or the publisher.

Under no circumstances will any blame or legal responsibility be held against the publisher, or author, for any damages, reparation, or monetary loss due to the information contained within this book. Either directly or indirectly.

Legal Notice:

This book is copyright protected. This book is only for personal use. You cannot amend, distribute, sell, use, quote or paraphrase any part, or the content within this book, without the consent of the author or publisher.

Disclaimer Notice:

Please note the information contained within this document is for educational and entertainment purposes only. All effort has been executed to present accurate, up to date, and reliable, complete information. No warranties of any kind are declared or implied. Readers acknowledge that the author is not engaging in the rendering of legal, financial, medical or professional advice. The content within this book has been derived from various sources. Please consult a licensed professional before attempting any techniques outlined in this book.

By reading this document, the reader agrees that under no circumstances is the author responsible for any losses, direct or indirect, which are incurred as a result of the use of information contained within this document, including, but not limited to, — errors, omissions, or inaccuracies.

Contents

Preface

The very first thing is to understand what social media marketing refers to and know how to use it. It is extremely important for any company to advertise themselves and their products and services. The best way to do so is by making use of social media platforms. You will see that it is possible for you to reach out to millions just by being part of a social media website.

The next thing to do is undertake the step by step procedure that you must adopt in order to arrive at the desired results. You have to go about it in a set way so that you can save on both time and effort. Start by researching the topic of social media marketing and then move to choosing the best platform for yourself. The next step is for you to set yourself up online and then look for the best promotional strategies that you can use to promote your products and services.

Facebook is one of the best platforms that you can pick to advertise your brand and products. You will see how easily you can reach out to millions. You have to make good use of Facebook pages and you will see that it is one of the best platforms to promote your brand and image. Facebook is an easy platform to advertise on and it is even simpler to keep it updated. You will find it quite convenient to tell people about your products and services by making use of Facebook pages.

The next social media platform that you can advertise on is Twitter. Twitter, as you know, is the second most used social media platform in the world. You can keep it small and simple and advertise your brand, products and services. You can easy link all your social media platforms using this medium. You have to post Instagram pics on your twitter account and get people to notice it. You have to know how to use the #s and participate in the on-going viral movement and capitalize upon it.

YouTube is the next social media platform that you can use to advertise your company, products and services. YouTube gives you the chance to make use of videos that you can upload and reach out to customers. YouTube videos have the tendency to go viral, which will make it extremely easy for you to promote yourself. YouTube also has the power to demonstrate your products and services to your customers, which you should use to your advantage.

Instagram allows you to click pictures and upload them. These pictures need to be good quality pictures that you can use to promote your products and services. You have to appeal to as many people as possible if you wish to make the most of the platform. You have to get someone famous to endorse for you as that will get you noticed by a lot of people. Instagram is possibly the best platform for you to advertise and showcase your products as a picture speaks a thousand words.

We looked at the different dos and don'ts of social media marketing that you have to bear in mind. It is important that you understand them carefully and do only as is asked of you to. Over doing something will only hurt you and your company. Put in the right efforts and you will see that it is simple for you to appeal to the right audience and increase your customer base. You can go through the don'ts again and steer clear of them.

Remember that the customer is always king. When you keep them happy you will see that your business is growing in leaps and bounds. So, you have to listen to what they are saying and keep them satisfied. Don't unnecessarily fall into traps that some of the customers or non-customers will set up. They will only be interested in pestering you and not really interested in buying any of your products and services. You have to learn to turn a blind eye to such people and continue with interacting with all your best customers.

You have to organize events for your best customers in order to understand them better and also keep them happy. The event needs to be good in order to keep the audience interested and educate as many new people about it as possible.

You have to focus on the offers that you organize for these people as that has the capacity to pull your audience in and keep them interested. Try to be as unique with your offers as possible and be creative.

There are other types of social networking sites that you can work with to promote your company. These include linked in, Google+ etc. All of these will help you reach out to a bigger and diverse audience. After all, isn't that what you want? A big audience that will keep your business going for a long time, so you have to put in an effort to be present on all the platforms that exist on the Internet and diversify your presence.

Introduction

When it comes to marketing your brand, products and services, you have to be as innovative as possible to remain on top of your game; given the amount of competition that exists out there, you have to be the best to make it big. If you settle for something mediocre or choose a beaten path, then you and your company will probably go unnoticed.

Ask any marketing expert about it and they will point to how it all boils down to making smart choices with your marketing strategies and trying to beat out the competition by being as innovative as possible.

It is of course easier said than done and you have to put in the effort to make all the right choices for your company. Given the plethora of options out there, it is obvious that you will need a little help; especially if you are your company's own PR manager.

One of the best, and most preferred, ways to advertise your products, and reach out to millions of customers worldwide, is by making use of Social Media. As you know, the Internet plays host to billions of people worldwide and you can easily reach out to many of them just by tapping into the different social media avenues.

In this book, we will look at how you can do so with ease and make your presence felt on all the different social media platforms. We will look at the individual media platforms in detail and understand why they are great choices for you and your company.

The main goal will be to beat your competition and stay ahead of the herd.

I thank you for choosing this book and hope you enjoy it.

Chapter 1: Why Social Media For Your Brand in 2019

Social media refers to various platforms that are available on the Internet, which provide users the chance to create their profiles and share and promote content. These social media platforms are all designed to help people and companies establish a social presence and let others know about their products and services.

The popularity of social media, as a marketing tool, rose in the last decade as more and more companies realized its true potential and began using it to their advantage. They understood that it is possible for them to reach out to millions of people, worldwide, and increase their customer base by several folds.

Social media is now part of every company's marketing strategy. Right from a small store in Japan to a multi-million dollar company in the US, everybody is using the power of the Internet to get noticed and improve their product's sales.

Through the course of this book, you will understand the real use of social media in terms of your marketing strategy and why it is extremely important for you to have a strong marketing plan in place in order to promote your products and services.

Let us now look at why social media is useful.

Personal Branding Secrets for 2019

Networking on social media seems simple enough: you create an account, you post a few times, and you get comments, right? Wrong. Social media is rapidly evolving and the networking front needs to be done with far more intimate strategies now. If you want to have a strong reputation built on social media, you need to be incorporating many different styles of sharing, engaging, and interacting with your audience. This means taking advantage of the many different features available on social media platforms, as well as spreading out and covering multiple different platforms. The more you spread out and the more you engage, the more you will become known by your audience. This is how you will create a reputation, build relationships, and maximize your success in 2019.

If you truly want to create your mark of success in today's world, you need to know how to stand out from the rest of the crowd. With virtually everyone being exposed to a global markets' worth of faces and profiles, standing out is the only way to be recognized, stay fresh and relevant, and be seen by your desired audience. Doing so is not nearly as hard as you would think, though it does require you to understand how social media works, recognize the importance of the social aspect, and consistency. If you incorporate the many strategies shared within this book then you can guarantee one thing, your social media strategy for your personal brand will be strong and your capacity to become recognized by your desired audience and stay relevant will be inevitable.

In 2019, the competition is getting fiercer, but the strategies are evolving as well. With social media being around for more than 10 years now, people and businesses alike are well aware of how social media can be leveraged. As we shift into a more digitized world, taking advantage of this leverage can only mean great results for you.

The key differences of personal branding in 2019 will be based around how networking is done. In the past, individuals could build a reputation for themselves or their personal brands by networking at business meetings, socials, and gatherings. Many would attend dinners, charity events, and other networking socials to meet other business-minded folk and build a reputation for them that allowed them to become recognized and well-known for who they were. While these aspects have not changed, the online front has given individuals a much wider platform to work with.

Now, personal brands can be managed online through the same key skills: networking and socializing.

How Social Media Marketing Works In 2019

In order to become successful b making use of social media marketing you really need to get yourself better acquainted with the complex hierarchy that exists and the workings of these platforms. Like it is the case with any online marketing strategy, even in the case of social media marketing it will all have to start with you and your website. Your website will act as the foundation, the base on which you can start building your campaign. Blogs have been gaining a lot of publicity, if your website has one then that's good and if it doesn't then perhaps it's time that you have added one. Blogs will enable you to provide regular steams of content that will help you grab and then hold on to the attention of your audience and in order to increase the number of people who are subscribing to your website, increase the number of followers you have got on any social media platforms and for also giving your business a sound online presence, a blog will really come in handy.

You probably would have come across the term RSS feeds and you might have even used them. If you haven't done so, then you probably should. RSS stands for Really Short Simple Syndication. RSS is really a great tool that can help you sort your content out in a way that provides you with the option of personalization. The benefit of personalization is that you can sort your content according to different sectors and areas of interest of your audience. People can always subscribe to your website and they can always agree to receive the RSS feed that will let them view the content as well as let them know of any updates. When you can personalize the information available you can filter it depending upon the requirements of your target audience.

Then there is the option of bookmarking as well as social sharing. This can be thought of as the process that lets you tag people and also keys you share certain elements of the content you have got on various social networking sites such as Facebook, Twitter and even Google+ or even on social bookmark sites such as Delicious, Digg or even StumbleUpon. If you really want this to work, then you will have to ensure that the content that you are wanting to post is of high quality and is relevant to the audience. It really won't work if you are just sharing silly memes or GIFs. If your audience doesn't think the content that you are posting is relevant then it is highly likely that they will stop following you.

Social search tools will also be really helpful. Google Places, Foursquare, Yelp and even Bing Places are some of the popular directories that are available online and you can get yourself listed on these sites. So that when anyone is searching for your name then your listed address would come up on the search. This will help you draw more attention to yourself and will help you in strengthening your online presence which is really crucial for your business. Social search tools are highly recommended by me and this will help in acting as a catalyst for improving the publicity for your business.

Which social media platform to make use of?

There are very few people who wouldn't have heard of Facebook or Twitter, but these aren't your only options there are a variety of social media platforms that you can make use of. If you can make use of it in the right way then your marketing campaign will be successful.

Facebook

It is a unanimous opinion that **Facebook** is the most popular social media platform. There are more than 1.2 billion active users on Facebook. This platform provides you with an opportunity to advertise about different kinds of businesses it can be paid or free advertising. It also provides you with the option of creating pages dedicated solely to your business and this can help you engage your potential customers. Facebook ads work according to PPC model that allows you to target certain ads and specific audiences. You can also share your content and communicate with your audience on a personal level.

Instagram

Instagram is another popular social media site that is aimed at social media; it can be either in the form of photographs or even videos. This site has over 150 million active users and it has become the latest fad irrespective of their age. This is a perfect option for all those businesses that rely heavily on visual media like fashion businesses, food, design, and travel and so on. Businesses can opt for either posting photos or videos of their products on Instagram and they can organize different photo or video contests for spreading publicity about their business. You can link your Instagram account to a business website but you can mention the same in any of your posts on other social media sites as well. You can make use of Instagram for generating web traffic for your website and thereby generate more interest.

Twitter

Twitter is all about Microblogging and it is a networking platform where there are more than 200 million active users. This is considered to be a very popular platform for businesses, celebrities and entrepreneurs alike. Twitter users can post updates and these are known as tweets. A tweet cannot be more than 140 characters long and this condition gives twitter the feel of an SMS system. You can create your business stage and you can make use of this for attracting your customers as well as getting updates to your audience without much trouble. You can also make use of the promoted tweets feature that gives you access to paid advertising and you can reach a much wider audience by making use of this.

Google+

Google+ has more than 540 million active accounts and this is considered to be the second largest social media site in this world. It is fully integrated with a lot of other services that Google offers and it is a really good option for businesses as well as individuals who are looking for a platform for their soul a media marketing strategy. This is a professional platform and it aims at businesses by allowing them to form relationships with their customers, investors and other interested parties. Your profile on Google+ will be linked to all other Google services that you make use of such as Google places.

LinkedIn

LinkedIn has more than 270 million active users and this is aimed for businesses alone. This is an incredible platform for anyone who is associated with the business world. Unlike all the other social media networking sites that cater to both businesses as well as individual users, LinkedIn solely caters to different businesses. Using this platform you can create a Company Page and this gives you the opportunity to showcase how well your company is doing and it also gives you a means of reaching out to your potential customers. This really should be your go to website if you want to develop your business connections, especially if you are involved in Business-to-Business marketing. This will allow you to find as well as hire employees or even search for any business leads by going through different profiles of likeminded people or people with similar interests.

Pinterest

Pinterest is not just a website where people get to pin photos. It is so much more than that. This is a unique platform it is not like any other social media sites and also social media marketing. This has around 70 million active users at present, making it a relative teenager in terms of its popularity but that number has been increasing at a steady pace. This is the place for both business users as well as individuals particularly those who make use of a lot of visual media. This would be for businesses that are related to the fashion industry like jewelry designers, photographers, any designers or basically any business that heavily relies on visual media. Pinterest also offers business accounts that come with added features that will let you analyze your pins and also help in promoting particular pins. Your business profile can also be easily synced with your accounts on other sites such as Facebook or even Twitter.

YouTube

In a strict sense YouTube really isn't a social media site but then it is the most visited video sharing site in the world and also the third most frequently visited site as well. **YouTube** combines a lot of features that make this site a vital tool to make use of in your social media marketing strategy. This is a free platform that anyone can access and you can make use of this site for publishing any videos that are related to your business or area of interest. You can also make use of the feature of paid advertising for promoting your products or services and this means that your ads would show up on videos that are posted by other users as well.

Why is social media useful for marketing?

Social media holds a lot of potential and will help in increasing your customer base. You will see how easy it is for you to reach out to different customers that are based all over the world. Let us now look at some of its real uses to companies.

SEO

You can make use of SEO when you set up an online account. SEO stands for search engine optimization, which will help you get noticed. You can use it to your advantage and turn up as the first search result online. That will ensure that your page gets visited more often, which will mean more customers for your business.

These form just some of the benefits of using social media for marketing but are not limited to just these. As and when you start using social media you will be acquainted with the other benefits. Following are the likely benefits and the reasons why you should start making use of social media marketing right now.

Reach

The first and most important use is the reach that this platform provides to its users. You will see that it is possible for you to reach out to more people just by making your presence felt on these sites. When you add one person, you will automatically end up adding another 10. This is not possible when you advertise in the traditional way. You will hardly be able to reach a few hundred there whereas here, you can easily reach millions just by clicking a few buttons and uploading pictures of your products and services.

Recognition

Your brand recognition will grow in leaps and bounds. Imagine having a small shop in a remote island and trying to reach out to the world. It will seem like a herculean task. But now, you can easily reach out and have our brand successfully recognized by million just by setting up an account on a social media platform. It is like getting to set up free billboards on every street in the world. Your brand is sure to be recognized by millions around the world and you will see that it is possible for you to become a global image by establishing your presence on social media.

Costs

The costs of marketing can be considerably reduced when you take up online marketing. When you market in the traditional way, you end up spending a lot of money. Right from paying the advertising company to paying for the different promotional campaigns, there are many costs that will keep accumulating. You have to set up a big fund for it and only then will you be able to afford the traditional method of marketing. However, with social media, all of that can be reduced to a bare minimum. You will see that it is possible for you to promote your products and services with a very small to no budget at all! Imagine the kind of money you can save on just by adopting social media for your marketing needs.

Interaction

Through social media platforms, you can interact with many people including your customers and potential business partners. You can bring everyone under the same roof and allow them to interact with each other. You will see that it is easy for you to answer any queries that these people have towards your company, products or services and make it an interactive session. This type of a setting will go a long way in helping you establish a good connection with your customer base.

Conversion

Through social media, you can easily convert people into your customers. Now say for example 500 visit your page on a daily basis. Out of those, maybe 200 are your existing customers and the rest are new people. If even half of them, meaning 150 people convert into customers then you will now have 200+150 customers for your products. That is a great number for you to work with, especially when you are just starting out. That number will only grow over time and before you know it, you will have a big audience base following you.

Helps in improving your brand authority:

You shouldn't forget the basic of marketing just because you are making use of social media. You will have to keep interacting with your customers on a regular basis and when you do this it shows good faith towards not just your existing customers but your potential customers as well. With the advent of technology people these days like to brag or even criticize about a particular service or product on various social media platforms. And when they do happen to post about a particular brand online, they are in fact introducing this brand to several others on an indirect manner and this expands your audience base. As the number of people who are talking about your brand starts to increase then the publicity of your brand will increase too and it will be perceived as being more valuable. You can always tie up with individuals who are quite popular on social networking sites for the promotion of your product. This will help in increasing the publicity of your product manifold.

The inbound traffic increases:

Your inbound traffic is generally restricted only to your existing customers and all those users who would have searched for the keywords that currently work for your product or brand. But social media can really help you turn things around. Every profile that you manage to add on social media will help you create a pub that will directly lead to your website and you every piece of content that you have managed to acquire I'd an opportunity for attracting new customers. When the quality of the content that you make use of or publish on social media strata improving then it will also help in increasing the chance of generating conversions will also improve.

Reduction in the marketing costs:

According to an online report published by Hubpost, approximately 84% of all the marketers had to put in just around six hours every week and they had managed to generate a noticeable increase in their web traffic. Six hours is comparatively a very small price to pay for the more than proportional increase in your brand recognition. A little bit of effort can help you reap the benefits of social media marketing. Even if you are able to spend maybe an hour everyday for developing your content as well as designing the strategy for marketing, you will be able to see results in no time. The option of paid advertising can always be opted for, but whether or not you want to make use of it solely depends upon your goals. You needn't worry about started out small, it needn't be on a large scale and you needn't exceed your predefined budget. Once you have acquired an understanding of how social media marketing works, you can slowly start increasing your budget according to your needs and you will definitely be able to improve your conversion rate.

Better search engine rankings as well:

SEO can be thought if as one of the best and simplest manner in which you will be able to capture traffic that is relevant to your content and then direct such traffic towards your website. The requirements of this mode keep on changing constantly. It is not just about regularly updated the content on your blog, the optimization of the titles used and the distribution of such links that all lead back to your website. Most of the search engines tend to make use of social media presence for calculating their rankings and most of the established brands also tend to make use of social media in one form of the other. Just being active on social media is sufficient to send a signal of credibility to the search engines regarding your brand. To put it in a nutshell, if you really want your brand rankings to go up then you will need to have a really strong presence on various social networking platforms.

Better customer experience:

Social marketing is a channel of communication that really isn't much different from the traditional channels of communication such as phone calls or even emails. Every interaction that you might have with a customer on social media should be considered as an opportunity for you to promote your brand and you can do this by projecting a good customer service experience and it also facilitates in helping you to enrich the existing customer relationship. If at all a situation arises wherein a customer has taken to Twitter to express their grievance about any particular product then you should be able to take an immediate action and rectify the problem as well as apologize to them in the same public forum. But not all of your experiences are going to be negative. If any customer expresses their satisfaction and happiness with your product then you can express your gratitude to them and you can also provide them with a list of additional products that you would recommend. You should make use of social media for improving personal communication with your customers thereby providing them a personalized experience.

Improvement in customer insights:

Social media can prove to be really helpful because it also provides you with an opportunity to understand how the customers behave and this can be done through something that is referred to as social listening. You can do this by opting to monitor the comments that your customers might post; this would give you an insight into their personality and what they think of your business. Another thing you can do is opting to segment the syndicated content and this will let you understand the content that has been able to generate the most interest and according to this you will be able to post further related content. Not just this but you can also measure your rate of conversion depending upon the different promotions that you managed to post on different social networking platforms. Being able to determine the most used social media by your customers will let you understand the media channel that you should actually make use of. You can really make a move to improve your revenue if you know what exactly your customer wants.

The above-mentioned are the benefits that you can derive by making use of social media marketing. Bet if you really aren't fully convinced even now about making use of it; then here are some other things that you should really consider before writing it off.

The sooner the better:

The foundation on which social media marketing is based is relationship building and you can always do this by trying to expand your followers. This will help you attract more and more customers. The sooner you start the greater will be the number of audience whom you can attract.

Needn't worry about potential losses:

If you really think about it, then you will realize that there really won't be any losses that you will be incurring. The amount of time and money that you will be spending will be an insignificant fragment when compared to the potential profits that you can make. You don't necessarily have much to lose by making use of this but you do have a lot to gain. All you need to do is put in a few hours of work and spend a couple of hundred of dollars for getting started. This is all the investment that you need to make and you will definitely be able to reap way more than you will have to invest.

You really shouldn't be waiting any longer and should get started as soon as you can. The more you wait the higher are your chances of losing out on potential business. Social media marketing can really come in handy and help you attract a lot of customers and it can also help in improving your conversion rate. So, all you need to do is get started. Take the first step and jump onto the bandwagon, because whatever the cynics might say, social media marketing is here to stay.

Chapter 2: Building A Personal Brand in 2019

Building your personal brand will require three primary things: a vision, a strategy, and motivation. As long as you know exactly what you are creating, you have a strong strategy to create it, and you are motivated to the cause, you can create a powerful personal brand that will be recognizable and admirable.

The thing about personal brands is that they are not just business-oriented, they are *personal.* This means that your personal brand needs to be integrated into your own vision for your own life, as the two will be one and the same in the long-run. That being said, the rest of this chapter is going to support you in understanding how you can build your personal vision and what will be required to support you in designing your personal core strategy. We will also explore what will motivate you to keep you focused and on track so that you can have a strong foundation to support you in going forward.

Building Your Vision

The first step to building your personal brand is building your vision. For a standard business model, one would create a mission statement, outline their values, and determine what their overall vision was. This vision would be designed to incorporate their idea of where they would be 1, 2, 5, and 10+ years down the road. Doing the same for your personal brand is a must, as this gives you a clear direction to move in. When you know where you are going, creating your strategy and taking action is much easier.

Building your vision for your personal brand ultimately requires you to determine how you want your life to look. Since this is your personal brand, you need to look at it from a personal point of view. Consider what you want all aspects of your life to look like and how your brand fits into that. For example, if you want to travel a lot and running a travel company is your ideal brand, then you can clearly see that these two will work well together, and you can design your entire brand around travel. If you are more of a homebody and you love creating products or services, you can pick your favorite types of products or services to create and brand yourself in that particular field. Ultimately, your vision and your brand need to coincide.

When you know what you want for yourself and what your top priorities are in life for both now and later in the future, it becomes easier to brand yourself. For this part, there are no right or wrong answers. All you are doing is creating a vision and determining what you truly like the most about that vision.

To build your vision, follow the steps below. This will help you understand who you are, what you want, and what you are working toward in life.

Determine and Prioritize Your Values

Before you can identify what your personal brand is, you need to know what your values are. This is how you can determine what matters to you and how things need to look in order for you to truly feel satisfied in your life. Many people will overlook their true values and dream up a life fed to them by society. As a result, they may find themselves struggling to stay committed to anything or feeling like an imposter in their own life because they are living out of alignment with their values. Staying clear on and true to your values will do you a world of wonders in your life. Not only does it keep you feeling aligned and focused, but it also gives those paying attention to your brand a clear and authentic understanding of what matters to you. Believe it or not, if you attempt to work against your values, this discrepancy will be picked up on by many and it can take away from your reputation. Our values are things we are generally very focused on, concerned with, and passionate about so it can be very clear when we are not living in alignment with them.

Your values are the things that matter most in your life. Values often revolve around family, friends, community, ambitions, intelligence and knowledge, charity, important causes, and other such things. In essence, your values are anything that you regard in high value and feel are important in your life. These are the things that you consider "deal breakers" in your life. For example, say you hold family and – in particular – quality time with your family to high importance. It is likely that you would not want to take a career that pulls you away from having quality time with your family on a regular basis. Our values determine what we want for ourselves as they help us discover what means the most to us and how we can structure our lives to honor those things.

Many people feel that having strong and honorable values is important. While it certainly is, it is also important that your values are true to you. For that reason, refrain from adding any values to your list that you do not personally feel attached to. These will muddy your list, take away from what you truly care about, and prevent you from staying motivated to your vision because your vision will ultimately be built on something that is meaningless to you.

Once you have determined what all of your values are, you need to prioritize them based on what is the most important to you. Knowing what your core values are (the ones that are most important to you) versus your other values is important. Your core values will be the first to be considered whenever you are making important decisions in your life. The rest will come into play, but not necessarily as "deal breakers."

Identify What Your Passions Are

Now, with a clear understanding of what your values are, you also need to identify your passions. Your passions are comprised of virtually anything that you love doing the most. These may overlap with your values, but they should also be different. Not all will overlap, and that is okay. Typically, your values will be more broad (i.e. "family"), but your passions will be more specific (i.e. "taking your family on vacations.") Passions should not just be interests, but things that you genuinely like doing and that you can stay committed to.

You should outline two sets of passions: personal passions and professional passions. Your personal passions should be everything you love doing in your personal time that helps you feel more fulfilled. Your professional passions should be the things that you love doing that have the capacity to add to your career or entrepreneurial pursuit.

When it comes to personal branding, you will want to talk about both types of passions. However, your professional passions should naturally be the predominantly discussed passions. This will not take away from your personal passions, but it will help you identify yourself based on a professional nature. Your personal passions can then be shared and discussed in a way that adds to the many layers of who you are and gives you depth for those who enjoy following you and interacting with you in the online space.

Determine Your Ideal Traits

Your next step in envisioning your personal brand is identifying what your traits are. Understanding what makes you who you are and recognizing what your key traits and characteristics help you to identify yourself. If you can easily identify yourself in a describable manner, then identifying yourself to others will be infinitely easier. Furthermore, you can choose to create a vision that compliments your traits, rather than attempt to create and commit to one that is completely misaligned for who you are.

You should ideally be outlining both your best traits and your flaws. This can help you understand what your strengths and weaknesses are, helping to guide you forward on your journey of understanding yourself and building your vision.

The traits that you incorporate in your outline should be measured. In other words, put them on a scale of 1-to-10, where 1 means you have that trait but only a small amount, and 10 means you have that trait to the maximum degree. This can help you understand who you are in a more accurate manner and help you determine whether your vision will actually fit with you or not.

Discuss With Those Closest to You

The last step in discovering who you are is talking with the people who are closest to you. Asking loved ones or close friends what they think of you and how they honestly identify you is a great way to discover how other people already see you. This means that you can verify if who you are and who you want to be or brand yourself as are aligned or not. Furthermore, it will support you in discovering how you can make the necessary adjustments to get to where you want to go.

Putting it All Together

Now that you have a clear understanding of who you are, what you value, and what you are passionate about, creating your vision should be easy. The first thing you need to do is discover what it is that you have done in your life that has felt the most rewarding and that was aligned with your values and passions. This can help you discover what has been the most enjoyable and fun aspects of your life that also brought you a great reward. It is likely that your end vision will incorporate some of these activities.

The next thing you need to do is narrow down which of those activities were the most enjoyable and most rewarding. That way, you can discover what *specifically* you want to do. Then, you want to discover what your ideal outcome would be. In other words, what career would be the most enjoyable for you that would also create the results you desire in your life? Once you have, you can easily claim this as your end vision. All that is left to do is compare it against your values to make sure that it genuinely fits with your life and that it will be fulfilling in every aspect. Then, you can reverse-engineer it to get your near-future vision and to create the strategy for you to get there.

Chapter 3: Building Your Core Brand Strategy

Your core brand strategy involves the key aspects of your brand: your image, your identity, and your outreach. Your image can be summarized as how you visually present yourself. In a personal brand, this should include yourself personally, your sense of style, a symbol or logo to represent you, and a color scheme that will represent you. You can also create a branding package for yourself that includes a color palette, your chosen fonts, your logo, and some sample images that show both the look and feel of how you want your brand to look. With this package, you can use it to determine how everything will be shared with your audience. Creating this image-based brand package will ensure that your look is consistent and identifiable and that people know what to expect with you. Your image will be at the core, as people are going to visually identify you based on what you show them.

Creating multiple smaller milestones in this way not only identifies and outlines a strategy for you to get to your end-goal, but it also supports you in having a clear path for right now. Furthermore, these smaller goals mean that you can reassess your overall vision at each milestone and adjust your bigger strategy to make sure that you are truly aligned with this goal. While everyone would love for the drive from point A to point B to be extremely straightforward and clean cut, the reality is that many things will happen and change between now and then that will require you to adjust your strategy. Not becoming too attached to the long-term strategy and staying focused on what needs to be done to reach your next milestone on time is a great way to accommodate for these and to spend more time doing and achieving and less time planning and stalling. While a great vision is important, getting stuck on the vision and not taking any action will never help you achieve your goals.

Your identity is important as well. To secure your core strategy with your identity, you want to pay attention to keywords, catchphrases or mottos, your name, and your usernames and domain names across the internet. Before you begin branding yourself publicly, decide what you want people to look up when they are looking for you. Do you want them to search for your name directly, or do you have a name you want to be identified as? For example, you could brand yourself as "James Adams" or you could brand yourself as "The Soccer Dude." What you choose is entirely up to you. Just know that this name needs to stay with you the entire way. Once you have chosen it, secure your username across all social media platforms and as a domain name. This will ensure that as you grow out into your various outreach methods, your name remains consistent and therefore identifiable and easy to locate online. This means that your audience can easily follow you around. Purchasing and securing these beforehand is the best way to make sure that you do not begin branding yourself as one thing but later discover that the name is taken already on a different platform. That way, if you just want to start on one or two platforms before building out, you can.

The other aspect of your identity is who you are. The best way to secure this part of your core strategy is to write your ideal bio for yourself. However, write it as though you are someone else identifying yourself with another person. For example, "You should follow James Adams! He is a soccer announcer who is always sharing the latest soccer news, plus awesome jokes!" What you want to be known for needs to be considered in this way. That way, you can begin building yourself based on how you want others to identify you as well.

Lastly, your outreach is an important part of your core strategy. This is how you are going to actually get people to know who you are and what your image is. Your long-term outreach strategy should include the many different techniques and strategies outlined throughout this book. However, you may choose to design a starter strategy that is more manageable and effective for you. Attempting to master every single strategy at once can be overwhelming, thus making it a challenge for you to master any and potentially causing you to struggle to be seen at all. Instead, you want to identify how you want to begin your strategy and where you will go from there. Ideally, you should start on just one or two platforms online. Get the hang of these platforms and begin expanding your followers before moving to another platform to master those. This way, you can really get the hang of each one before moving on to the next. This type of strategy is more sustainable and will support you better in the long run.

What Motivates You

Lastly, a personal brand requires that you know how to motivate yourself. Simply put, you will not have the massive support in motivating yourself to move forward when it comes to personal branding that you might in other areas of your life where other people are concerned. Your personal brand is very personal to you and no one will care about it more than you do. If you are not able to motivate yourself to stay committed to your goals and keep moving forward, no one will be able to.

Knowing what motivates you and how you can keep yourself motivated is essential. Generally, we are motivated by our values and vision. However, there will be times that this simply does not feel like enough. Knowing how to create more instantaneous bursts of motivation, such as by setting shorter-term goals, rewarding yourself highly for reaching your goals, or celebrating yourself at each milestone can be a great way to keep yourself moving.

Another thing many people consider is their "why." Their why is essentially the reason why they are even doing what they are doing. Many people are motivated by their children, their families, their illnesses or disabilities, their living conditions, their desire for money or to travel, or otherwise. Knowing what exactly it is that you want and how your personal brand is going to get you there is a great way to keep yourself motivated in moving forward and building success.

As you identify what motivates you, be sure to write it down and keep it handy. Then, on those days that are particularly challenging and when you are unsure of what to do to keep yourself going, you can review the list and remember all of the ways that can keep you moving forward. That way, you will be sure to stay motivated, stay on track, and achieve your vision with your own support.

Chapter 4: Identify Yourself

The first step in this practice is to write out a list of everything that makes you different from the others. This includes any quirk, trait, flaw, passion, or piece of your personal history that is unique from others' experiences.

This list is going to help you discover what is different about you that virtually no one else can claim or identify with. Although you will obviously share overlapping traits with others, this particular list is entirely unique to you. Seeing it out on a list will help you recognize how different you are and what stands you apart from others. It will also help you determine which of these may actually support you in your personal branding. Be sure to include everything on this list, even the items that seem unimportant. You may later come to realize that they are actually very important elements to add into your unique *you*-based brand!

With your list completed, prioritize what items on the list you identify with the most. This will help you see what is most prominent in making you uniquely you and what is least. This can be prioritized based on what is the most different or unique, and what is the most common in your personality.

Your Vision

Now, with your list completed and prioritized, you can blend it with your vision. To do this, determine what traits actually support you in reaching your vision. For example, if you want to be known for making the best bread in the world and you have a preference for keeping your kitchen *just so* or you favor one particular ingredient in your bread over anything else, this can be unique to you. Highlighting and amplifying this can make it much easier for you to discover what makes you different from anyone else and how this sets you apart from the rest of the crowd. It also supports you in knowing which of your unique aspects blends best with your vision, helping you to actually use these characteristics as marketable traits.

Now, you want to identify yourself once again. If you will recall, in chapter 3, you were encouraged to introduce yourself to someone else as though you were not actually yourself. So, pretend that you are your own follower and that you are telling a friend about your account. How would you identify yourself and how would this particular quirk or trait tie into that description? Are you the witty bread maker? The sarcastic shoe cobbler? The heroic horse whisperer? The soccer dad who loves making dad jokes? What is your identity?

Once you know how you want to be identified, you can easily begin building your personal brand around this persona. In this aspect, you want to remain true to who you are, but you are being more selective about which aspects of yourself you are going to amplify the most. The reason is that these particular aspects of yourself are the ones that are going to set you apart, thus making you more likely to be noticed and picked apart from others in the same space as you.

With this identification, you want to tie in all of your marketing around it. Any time you are writing content, sharing images, or otherwise interacting with your audience, look for a way to tie these particular traits in with your brand. There will likely be more than one as people are multifaceted and you do not want to come across as dense or boring, so take advantage of this and share all of the quirks, parts of your history, traits, and flaws that make you unique and overlap with your vision. This helps people get to know you more intimately, gives you a great angle to share from, and builds the relationships between you and your audience.

Chapter 5: Create Your Offer

Attempting to gain the interest and attention of everyone is only going to ensure that you are not successful in being seen or recognized in the online space. Your better objective is to pay attention to who you specifically want to be liked by and focus on building your brand around catering to them. A great way to begin identifying who you actually want to spend time with and who your ideal audience is would be to imagine the following scenario and consider your answer:

You walk into a social gathering that has gathered around your favorite topic. Immediately, you notice three groups of people. Upon taking a moment to notice each group, you decide which one you feel the most attracted to and decide to walk up to them and begin engaging in a conversation with them. The question is: who are they, what attracted you to them, and what are you hoping to engage in with them?

By identifying the answer to the above scenario-based question, you get a solid idea of who you actually like and who interests you the most. Remember, your personal brand needs to be personal to you. Attempting to appeal to an audience that does not actually resonate with you will likely only result in you feeling like an outcast because you struggle to fit in effectively. Instead, you want to identify where you fit in. If where you currently fit in and where you want to fit in is different, this is a great opportunity to practice self-development so that you can begin fitting in with your desired audience. In that case, choose your desired audience or the one that you personally would like to be acquainted with the most and honor this personal growth in yourself.

Once you have a better idea of who you want to be in your audience, you need to actually define your target audience. This means that you need to get very specific on what the demographic, who is in the audience, and why you are both interested in engaging with each other. You also need to determine how you are going to approach them and create a relationship with them since they presently have no idea who you are and you are the one wanting to build the relationship.

There are three steps in creating your audience and then recognizing who they are. Remember that in business, who you want to be your audience and who they actually are can change. Even in personal branding. This means that as you go on with the strategies in this chapter, you might find that the people responding best to your content are completely different from who you anticipated. In this case, there are two things you can do: adjust your ideal target audience or adjust your strategy. If you are happy with the response you are getting, adjusting your ideal audience grants you the opportunity to carry on with the momentum you are already building. If you are feeling completely unhappy with the audience you are currently targeting, adjusting your strategy is a good way to help yourself appeal to the audience you prefer. That being said, make sure that any adjustments you make still align with your values and vision so that you do not stray away from who you truly are in favor of appealing to your ideal person.

Empathize With Your Audience

The first step in identifying your audience is empathizing with them. If you have an idea of who you are targeting, you can begin discussing topics and challenges that resonate with this ideal audience. Be crystal-clear in establishing empathy toward this audience, letting them know that you identify with what their problems are and you understand why they are such a challenge. This supports you in building relationships with your audience and begins to identify you as "one of them."

You can easily empathize with your audience through your social media platforms, as well as anywhere else that you are presently performing outreach such as on your blog, in email newsletters, in forums, or anywhere else.

In addition to showing your audience that you identify with them and that they can relate to you and vice versa, empathizing with your audience also begins discussions. By engaging in these discussions, you can determine exactly what it is that these people are identifying with, what their hopes and dreams are, what they are looking for, and how your personal brand might be able to better serve them. In this case, it is not only a great way to define your target audience, but also to begin creating a business that will serve them.

Create Your Offer

The next step in building your personal brand, making sales, and defining your target audience is creating a customized offer for the audience you identified in step one. This customized offer should be based on everything you learned about your audience, supporting you in creating an offer that directly supports them in having their needs met. This means that they are more likely to be interested in your offer, thus helping you maximize your engagement and make sales right off the bat.

This offer is going to do three things for you: increase exposure, earn sales, and perform market research. Through this offer, you are going to have people purchasing from you as long as you have crafted it correctly based on your demographic. The most important aspect of all of this, however, is that you are going to see exactly who within your overall demographic is actually purchasing what you are creating for them. This particular demographic will be far more defined, making *them* the ones you want to cater to. For example, if you know that moms in their 20s and 30s are your primary demographic but that moms between the ages of 28-34 who have more than one kid are your biggest purchasing audience, then you know specifically who you want to cater your brand toward. This goes for any audience. The more defined audience will be drawn not from those who engage the most, but from those who are actually willing to purchase from you.

If you are not yet ready to make sales, you might consider making a free offer that allows people to join you in an online live event, download something you have made for them, or otherwise engage with you in a way that requires for them to actually commit to something. This particular will not earn you money nor will it give you an exact idea of who is willing to pay for your content versus who is simply willing to accept the free offer, but it will give you a stronger idea of the demographic you are targeting. This is a great idea if you are not yet ready to design an offer or if you are still trying to navigate the waters in which you are wading.

Improve Exposure and Conversions

The analytics you draw in through your sales are going to tell you who you are targeting that are actually purchasing from you. Through this information, you can begin refining your outreach to increase your effectiveness at reaching your ideal target client and converting them into customers. This process of refining your outreach and monitoring your analytics is the best way to see who responds best to you and how you can get them to respond even better. Through this action, more information regarding your target client will begin appearing in your analytics and you can get even better at relating to them, identifying the problems that they are having, and creating solutions that you can sell them.

Creating Your Audience "Profile"

With the analytics rolling in from your previous offer and the conversions that you have made, you will want to begin creating your audience's profile. This will essentially be a specific profile of who is in your audience, what defines them, what their motivations are, any opportunities you have to serve them, and what you can do to serve them better. Knowing this person specifically and doing all that you can to understand them ensures that you know exactly who you are talking to and how you should be talking to them in order to help them resonate better with you.

The best way to do this is to create an identity profile that outlines one specific person in your audience. This person should be the ideal character that defines who you are talking to, thus making them the "mascot" of your audience. For that reason, they do not need to be a real person. Instead, they can be a profile you create based on the summary of all of the information that you are learning through the audience.

You should also include anything relevant to what you are doing. For example, if you are creating a family-based brand, you would want to include information about the age range of the family, whether the parents are together or not, how many children they have, and anything else relevant to what you are aiming to do.

The more you detail your description of your ideal audience and understand who they are and why this makes them ideal for your brand, the easier it will be for you to identify how you can share with them. Be specific and include anything that you think will be relevant.

Some people will even include a name and an ideal image of who their audience looks like, typically found in a stock image on Google. This can be helpful in supporting you in narrating a dialogue between yourself and your audience, but it is not necessary. If you do choose to do this, keep the image handy and any time you are going to share something with your audience, run it by your ideal profile. See how the information serves them, whether or not it supports you in generating success, and if you can do anything to have a more effective interaction.

Identify Your Opportunity to Serve

Now that you have identified your audience, you need to define their problems and look for opportunities to serve them. Looking at who they are and determining their likely needs based off of their profile are a great way to begin understanding what your audience needs and how you can fulfill that need. You can then go ahead and begin creating opportunities for yourself.

For example, say your audience is the elderly people who are struggling to get around their house. You identify that they are likely those who are mostly living on their own with success but that their mobility is an issue. Their need, then, is being able to move around on their own while feeling safe and steady. That way, they can continue to live on their own for much longer. Your opportunity would be to create a solution to serve their mobility needs, whether it be selling products that make their mobility safer or designing a service that allows a support aid to come to their house on a set schedule to support them in accomplishing the tasks that require more mobility than they can comfortably handle.

When you know who your audience is and what they need, you can create products or services that support them in having that best life. This will help guarantee your sales. The understanding of all of this information will support you in creating a strong brand that supports you in getting those sales, however.

Chpater 6: Branding on Instagram in 2019

Getting on Instagram gives you a great opportunity to take advantage of creating a more personalized, visual brand in a sometimes cold and segregated community. For a long time, social media was known as being impersonal and disconnected because of the very nature that people were not getting together and networking in a powerful way. Adding in the visual element and taking advantage of the growing trend of creating genuine engagement between you and your audience is the main objective of Instagram especially in 2019, and Instagram provides you with all of the necessary tools to create this connection and develop this relationship.

Another reason why getting on Instagram is important to your brand is that many of Instagram's users actually use the platform to locate companies and influencers that are representing "the small guy." In other words, many are looking to get away from supporting faceless, soulless corporate structures and begin supporting individuals, small companies, and local businesses. By getting yourself on

Instagram, you put yourself directly in front of an audience who is looking for exactly what and who you are. This means that not only do you have a demographic perfectly suited to your target, but you also have one that is eagerly ready to consume any content you are putting out for them.

The big key in social media in 2019, as you are now well aware of, is being authentic and sharing the real aspects of who you are. That being said, it is no surprise that Instagram is going to really be a strong tool for anyone who shows up and shares in an authentic manner. The fact of the matter is that there are hundreds of thousands of photographs out there that all look basically the same, just like the different models or people in them. While it is incredible to see everyone sharing, it has led to a desensitization of sorts in the world of Instagram. Many people find themselves scrolling these images just for pure pleasure and rarely actually following the accounts or engaging with them. This is because there are simply too many and none stand out enough to really make them worth following over the others. Instead, if they like the aesthetics, they will simply follow the hashtag (a feature that was newly introduced in 2018.) To avoid getting ignored in favor of a hashtag, make sure that you let your authenticity actually shine through in your images. While high-quality images and high-resolution photography is a must, doing the same thing everyone else is doing should be avoided at all costs.

At one time, everything was done with the intention of having the most likes and follows, but this time is long gone. Most potential followers and eventual customers do not give any concern to the number of followers or likes a person accumulates on social media. Instead, they want to see that your content and the things you are sharing are genuine and authentic. They should stand out, be different, and highlight those unique aspects of yourself that we covered in chapter 4. If you can fill your feed with images that represent yourself in an authentic, genuine, and unique manner, you will have far more luck in getting real followers who are sincerely there to support you and pay attention to what you are sharing. This means that your account will see far higher engagement and more conversions out of your followers turning into paying customers.

Step 1: Create the Ability to Get Seen

Lastly, you need to master the art of getting seen on Instagram, namely, hashtagging. Using hashtags on Instagram is the way that people are discovered. Instagram allows for each individual to tag up to 30 hashtags in their image, allowing you to use up to 30 popular tags that can expose you to tens of thousands, hundreds of thousands, or even millions of potential viewers. Using these tags properly can get you seen by a massive audience and can support you in getting far more follows and significantly more engagement.

There are two particular "rules" you need to follow when it comes to using hashtags on Instagram. The first rule is that you should never share the hashtags in the caption of your image *unless* it is a single extremely relevant one, or a custom one that you are using to help your audience engage with you. In this case, one or two is fine. However, the bulk of your hashtags should actually be placed within the first comment of your image within 30-45 seconds after posting your image. This ensures that your image gets engagement quickly, which supports Instagram's algorithm in pushing you up further in the feed so that you can get seen by a larger audience. That being said, you should pre-write your hashtag group out in a note on your phone then copy it so that as soon as you hit "share" on your image, you can instantly jump into the comments section and post your hashtags.

The second rule is that you never want to use hashtags that are barely seen, nor do you want to use hashtags that are overused. There are some exemptions here, however. For example, if you are working on using a particular hashtag to engage with your audience, then you have likely decided to use one that has never been used before. Creating your own in this way naturally means that no one else has used it, thus it is not seen often. This would be a fine usage of one that is rarely used. You can also use ones that are rarely used if they are very specific toward your audience. In this case, the few that do see the hashtags are far more likely to engage, making it worth it. When it comes to using overused hashtags, you want to avoid this as much as possible. Using 2-3 per post is okay, but any more than that and you are wasting your time. Hashtags that are overused are used many times per day, meaning you will quickly get buried and the window of opportunity is significantly smaller for you. Instead, you want to have your window of opportunity enlarged by using hashtags that have more than 75,000 posts per tag and less than 999,999. This ensures that it is used often enough that you will actually get seen, but not so often that you will get buried. Again, use up to 30 but at least 15 hashtags. This will ensure that you gain maximum exposure.

Step2: Create A Strong Instagram Strategy

On Instagram, the strategy is extremely necessary. Because of the nature of how "busy" the application is with so many users frequently uploading pictures and sharing them with the same hashtags that you are, you need to make sure that you are following specific practices to boost your profile and get greater exposure and engagement. The strategy you need will feature three steps: an attractive feed, consistency in posting, and regular genuine engagement.

Having an attractive feed will support you in being followed because, true to the nature of visual marketing, your audience cares about your aesthetic. This does not necessarily mean they are looking for a generic magazine-style feed. Instead, it means that they want something coherent, that looks good together as a whole, and that looks like you genuinely put thought into your posts. Downloading an app like PLANN which can support you in uploading images to your Instagram and dragging them into order to make them more aesthetically appealing is a great way to make your page more attractive. This makes it more interesting and engaging for the human eye, thus increasing your likelihood of individuals tapping "follow." The key here is making sure that you use the same filters, color schemes, and general lighting in your images. If you upload quotes, make sure they are based on a similar template that looks attractive as well.

Consistency is your next key. The general consensus is that posting three times per day will keep your feed active, at the top of peoples' pages, and easy to locate for new followers. This is a great rule of thumb, however, it is not entirely necessary. You may find that it is a challenge to discover and curate enough high-quality images to build a feed that rapidly. Depending on what you are posting, you can always draw stock images from websites like Unsplash or Pixabay, though this may take away from your authentic angle if you post too many. So, if you are choosing to tone it down in favor of having higher quality authentic content, you can lower your posting to just one or two times per day. The biggest key element here is posting on a daily basis. That being said, you do not want to go above three times per day as this can have you seen as spammy and can actually reduce your visibility and increase the number of unfollows you get.

Step 3: Take Advantage of Stories

Instagram has spread out into stories and IGTV as newer ways to share with your audience and help bring them into the behind-the-scenes of your life. These two unique sharing aspects allow you to engage with your audience in new ways, making it even easier for you to share and encourage followers to join you, watch you, and remember who you are.

Instagram stories are images or videos that you share that are only viewed for a few seconds and then completely disappear after 24 hours. However, Instagram also introduced something called "Story Archives" which appear on your profile. These archives are stories that you have saved and organized onto your profile in specific categories. Many brands are using them to share the key elements of their brands with other people. For example, if you are a fashion brand, you might have a "Fall 2019" category for archived stories. Then, any Fall fashion you spot can be snapped, added to your stories, and saved in a compiled list within the archive. This means that followers can see these archived stories whenever they want until you intentionally delete them.

Stories also offer two great marketing strategies that will help you dominate marketing in 2019. The first one is suspense marketing. Sharing images with your audience that gives a small insight as to what you are doing or what you are about to release without giving the full details or full demonstration is a great way to get people seeing what you are doing and have them start asking questions. The buildup of anticipation makes them far more interested and more likely to click to learn more when you finally launch or share whatever it is that you are actively in the process of launching.

Another way of marketing in your stories is through links. If you have 10,000+ followers, Instagram introduces a link-sharing feature that allows you to include clickable links in your stories. Viewers simply swipe up on the story and can see a link (or any links) that take them to whatever it is that they desire to see. This is a great way to market different things shown in your story or to market one specific thing in general. It is done by simply tapping the chain link icon that appears in the top right corner of your screen after reaching 10,000 followers on Instagram.

Instagram TV, or IGTV as the app calls it, is a video sharing feature that allows users to share videos up to an hour long that are stored on their channel. This channel can be comprised by any creator or Instagram user that chooses to upload content, allowing them to share anything they desire with their audience. Marketers and personal brands are using this to educate their audience, share new products through demonstrations, do "get ready with me" style videos, perform Q&A videos, and otherwise market through video sharing. This new tool has brought an entirely new layer of marketing to Instagram that has allowed personal brands to share far more, making it even easier to interact with and engage with your audience on Instagram while also providing valuable content that earns you greater followers. Anyone who follows you on Instagram can see your channel. You can upload to your channel directly through the Instagram app on your phone by tapping the IGTV icon on the top right corner of the main feed.

Step 4: Optimize Your Page's Branding

As with all profiles, you are going to want to optimize your Instagram account for your branding. When someone lands on your account, they should quickly be able to determine who you are, what you are doing, and what they can learn or gain from your account. This means that you need to have a username that reflects your brand, your name clearly displayed at the top of your page, a bio that explains what you do and what your personal mission is, any relevant link to find you elsewhere, and a feed that shows a visual of what you are sharing with other people on a regular basis.

Your name on Instagram is different from your username. Whereas your username is the name that people will use to find you, your name is what is displayed in bold font above your bio. Both the username and Instagram name need to be clearly displayed, easy to understand, and well-represented. Here is where having the same username across all social media platforms and your domain name already purchased is going to serve you. The username that you use should be what your brand is. If you yourself are your own brand, it should be your personal name. If your name is hard to spell, however, you might adjust it slightly and make that your brand. For example, Gary Vaynerchuk is a challenging name to spell so the famous influencer uses Gary Vee as his online persona to make him easier to recognize and find in the online space. If you have a brand name you are going by, or a title you identify with, you might use that instead. For example, "The Celestial Psychic" (@thecelestialpsychic) or "The Salad Spoon" (@thesaladspoon). Keep your username easy to spell and easy to identify. This will make it easy for people to find you and to remember you so that they can find you again. Your name, however, should simply be your first and last name. Again, that is unless your name is particularly challenging to spell, pronounce, or remember, then you may choose to swap it out in favor of an initial or a middle name.

The next thing you need to optimize is your profile image. This image should not be larger than what you see on your profile, so ideally it needs to be something that is easy to see in the small image. The best images for these profile shots are either headshots, a picture of your logo, or an image that captures what you share on your page and represents your "theme." Keep them clear and high resolution with a very clear focus, as this will ensure that your potential viewers are not confused by what they are seeing and overlooking your account thinking that you are just another user and not someone worthy of being seen.

Engaging With Your Followers

Your followers are the ones boosting your profile, liking your pictures, and giving your profile credibility. The more followers you get, the more you need to engage with them. Doing this is an extremely simple way of organically building relationships with your audience and supporting them in remembering who you are. It also shows potential followers that you care and that if they support you that you will be genuinely interested in developing a relationship back with them.

One obvious way to engage with followers is to comment back whenever they comment on your content. You should also search your brand's specific hashtag if you have one and like and comment on anyone who posts specifically about your brand. These particular people are going out of their way to share your brand, so rewarding them with attention and interaction is a great way to show your gratitude and thank them for their support.

You should also spend some time each day scrolling popular hashtags that are relevant to your business. Liking and, more importantly, commenting on other peoples' posts is a great way to get seen and increase the number of people paying attention to your page. It is important that you use genuine comments in this situation. Many businesses have come under fire recently for using pre-canned, generic "We love your page! Check ours out, too!" type comments that are seen as inauthentic and ingenuine by their audience. This gives your brand a spammy feel and can actually take away from the relationships you are building with your audience.

Instagram stories, Instagram live, and IGTV are three other features that give you a great opportunity to interact with your audience in a more live-in-the-flesh manner. Stories are always a great way to offer interesting, behind-the-scenes snippets of your day to your audience so that they can feel as though they are seeing into your life and genuinely building a relationship with you. If you run a brand that is identified on its own, you can focus the story on your employees and the goings on at your store or company.

Instagram stories also offer a unique feature to those with 10,000+ followers that allow you to attach links directly to your story. This means that you can advertise for a new product, service, blog post, or otherwise directly in your story and then inform watchers to "swipe up" to access the link and visit your link to purchase or further engage with your brand. This can be accessed by tapping the chain link icon in the top right corner of the screen when making stories and putting the link into the space provided. Again, this feature is only available to those with more than ten thousand followers.

Instagram live is a great way to offer live Q&A sessions, introductions, information, and other valuable, interesting, or entertaining tidbits to your audience in a way that allows you to directly communicate back and forth. Because it features your face and voice live on a video, it creates a more personalized and intimate connection between you and your audience.

IGTV is another great feature that was recently included. This particular feature works much like live but stays in the IGTV feed for 24 hours following your upload. It allows you to stay live for much longer, do more, and have a more professional look to your page. This is great for sharing tutorials, updating people on important happenings in your business, educating them, and otherwise sharing video-based marketing information in a more professional and new age manner.

Chapter 7: Personal Branding On Facebook in 2019

In 2019, Facebook is still the leading social media site in terms of having a large, diverse audience that can be tapped into for virtually anyone. Starting as a social media platform to connect friends and family across the globe to minimize the feelings of separation through the support of the internet, many have continued to use this platform for just that. Only, nowadays people are also using it as a powerful online networking tool. Features like groups, group chats, and pages are allowing individuals to connect with those they have never met before in a way that allows them to become friends and stay connected through the internet.

The one thing you really need to continue paying attention in 2019 is that everything you do in any form of public setting can be held against you on social media. This means that if you do anything that could take away from the personal brand that you are attempting to build and someone photographs you and shares it online, it is there for everyone to see. This is particularly troubling on Facebook where tagging can happen and virtually everyone has a profile so they can see your tags. For that reason, you need to be very cautious about who you spend your time with, where, and what you are doing. If you build your personal brand to authentically represent you, as we discussed in chapter 4, then you can feel confident that your reputation online and offline should continue to uphold and this should not be an issue.

Aside from having to make sure that you behave in a way that protects your reputation, Facebook gives you a vast and diverse platform to begin building your reputation organically. You can easily create a personal profile that you use for outreach, as well as a page and a group. There are so many unique tools available to you that you can use to begin engaging with others. As long as you use it properly, you can rapidly build your network, make meaningful connections, and begin building reputations not only between you and your audience but your brand and your audience as well.

Create a Friendly Profile

A profile, page or group needs to be friendly and engaging if you want people to actually want to befriend you or follow you online. Doing so requires three things: pictures that look friendly and open, content that is engaging and helpful, and an invitation or reason to follow you.

Your picture on Facebook should be something that clearly captures who you are and highlights your most notable feature. A great headshot, an image of you doing something you love such as taking photographs or spending time with your family, or a full body image of you all make for great pictures that can be used in your profile. The key importance here is to choose an image that is clear and high-quality, one that is illuminated enough that they can easily see the features on your face, and one that makes it very clear which person you are in the image.

Your content needs to be something that supports your ideal audience in immediately feeling as though they need to befriend, follow, or join you in the online space. Creating contents that are relevant, relatable, engaging, helpful, informative, entertaining, or inspirational is a great way to do just that. People like reading content with a purpose, especially when that purpose serves them, specifically. Keeping your content directed at serving others is a great way to give your audience a strong reason to add you as a friend, follow your page, or join your group on Facebook.

Lastly, you need to make it obvious that you *want* engagement from others. Particularly with personal profiles that are being used for branding and networking, people may feel confused as to whether or not they can add you. Making it obvious by adding a statement in your profile's bio on your personal page is a great way to encourage them to engage with you. If you want someone to follow your business page, you can always include a statement at the bottom of your posts that says "follow for more great content!" With groups, you can include a statement in the public group description that says something like "Join us for _____" so that you can identify who best fits within the group and invite that specific person to join you. This will work as a call to action, letting people know that you want to be engaged with and giving them the encouragement to do the same with you.

Building Your Reputation on Facebook

Building your reputation online is everything. Your reputation is going to be entirely based off of all of the information that you identified earlier in this book. Everything that you need to support your vision, connect with your audience, and make your personal goals will be incorporated. This can be identified within the identity you defined for yourself in chapter 4.

As you build your reputation, it is essential that you understand that every single interaction, engagement, and action you take on Facebook is going to serve this greater reputation. You cannot do anything online that would compromise this reputation and prevent you from being able to fulfill your goals by taking away from how others see you. This may sound intimidating, but it truly is not. The goal here is to make sure that you act in a way that is authentic and genuine toward who you are, what you desire to achieve, and how you share yourself with the world around you. Then, you need to be clear and concise in how you are sharing this with others.

Creating a reputation online, particularly on Facebook, will be defined based on where you spend your time, who you make friends with, and how you communicate with them. When you understand these three elements, it becomes much easier to create a strong reputation on your Facebook page.

Where you spend your time includes what pages and groups you are engaging in the most. If you are engaging in groups and pages that align with your vision and support your goals, you can easily share and network with people who are supportive. If you are engaging in areas that contradict your goals, however, you will quickly find yourself sullying your reputation by directly contradicting who you are trying to brand yourself as.

The friends you keep on Facebook matter, too. For example, if you are trying to brand yourself as a friendly and positive person but you have pessimistic and negative people regularly commenting on everything you share, this reflects negatively on you. To prevent this from happening, refrain from adding anyone who is in direct contradiction with your brand. If you cannot do this (say you do not want to hurt a family member's feelings), you can always adjust your privacy settings on your posts to exclude that particular person from seeing what you are sharing.

How you communicate with people includes what you are saying, what language you are using, and how you are supporting them. You want to keep this positive, on-brand, and supportive. The more helpful and kind you communicate, while also maintaining the right vernacular for your demographic, the more approachable and likable you will be by your desired audience. This will support you in creating a strong reputation for yourself that supports others in wanting to connect with you further.

Populate Your Information

On your Facebook page, a key part of branding is to make sure that you populate your profile, page, and group with plenty of information. The digital age has made people somewhat nosy, and they always want to know more. If people come across you and like what they see, they are going to want to browse your profile, page, and group to learn more about you. You need to have something for them to learn about! Boring pages that do not feature any interesting information informing them of who you are will result in the individual leaving your account once again because there is nothing to attract them and draw them in. However, an account with the "About" section filled out and more information about who you are, as well as a page and group with descriptions and stories fully filled out, give interested individuals plenty to read about. This means that they can learn plenty about you before actually deciding whether or not they want to engage with you.

It may seem heinous to have someone want to read everything about you first and then get to know you second, but this is how things work on Facebook. People are generally cautious about who they spend their time with, even online, and who they are willing to share their more personal information with. Having a profile that is well-populated with plenty of consumable information can help these individuals feel confident in choosing to communicate with you. It also helps them know what to expect. Furthermore, if you are selling products or services online, they may even find themselves interested and ready to purchase without ever having to go through the long process of getting to know you first. So, not only is this a great way to encourage networking by showing your audience that you are open and friendly, it also gives them a chance to see what you are all about and choose to purchase if they so desire.

Build Your Community

The last key strategy you need to pay attention to and nurture on Facebook in 2019 is your community. Groups are all the rage right now, and for good reason. When you run a group, it is your primary commitment to nurturing that group, share purposeful content that gives others a reason to stick around and facilitates the networking that goes on within the group. Building a community in this way gives people a great opportunity to get to know each other and yourself, and it puts you at the top of the community. This means that if everyone can only identify one single person in the group, it is pretty good that the one person they are identifying is you!

Update Frequently

Posting regularly is an essential way to stay relevant and connected with your audience. Ideally, you should be posting to Facebook about 3 times per day. You should also be spending a few minutes each day commenting, liking, and engaging with other people. This will be considered your networking time! Keeping your audience updated on what you are doing, sharing purposeful content, and engaging with your audience is the best way to make sure that you are regularly getting your name in front of them. That way, they can begin to identify who you are, understand what you are all about, gain value from you, and stay close with you online.

If you are networking in multiple areas on Facebook such as in profiles, pages, and groups, you want to spend time updating each of these unique areas. So, three updates on each of these three areas would suffice. This may sound like a lot, but it does not actually take long. Furthermore, you can always write or create inspired content ahead of time and schedule it to post to your account, page, or group using a third-party application like Hootsuite or Buffer. This is a great way to stay up-to-date without having to personally schedule aside fixed time each day to get online and update people. Then, all you have to do is make sure that you hop online to engage with people on a daily basis.

Going into 2019, the best way to keep people updated is through video marketing. People absolutely love videos that share great content by educating or entertaining them. Product demonstration videos, live Q&A videos, sharing a short clip of the goings on of your day or something relating to your brand, or otherwise sharing video content that supports your brand and reputation is a great way to take advantage of videos. Ideally, you should focus on creating professional and well-put-together videos as well as live videos that are filmed in real-time.

Another great area to share on in Facebook right now is stories. Facebook stories allow you to share exclusive, behind-the-scenes images of your life and brand with your audience. This helps bring them into your world and feel a greater connection to you, thus supporting you in having an even greater relationship with your audience. One great tip to know is that if you link your Instagram and Facebook together, you can share Instagram stories to your Facebook feed. This means that both audiences can be nurtured by the same story-sharing activity.

Chapter 8: Facebook Advertising for Your Brand in 2019

Once you have a strong idea of who your demographic is, Facebook offers many ways for you to begin interacting and engaging with your audience. You can choose many parameters for your advertisement, an objective, a budget, and the way it will look. It is important to understand that Facebook is better used for story marketing, sharing, and networking. Trying to facilitate hard sales on Facebook (i.e. "Toothbrushes - $2 each! Buy now!) will not work. People want to read, feel inspired, and take action.

Your Objective

Upon accessing your Ad Manager and selecting "Create Ad" you will be asked to choose your objective. Your objective section features 11 different objectives that you can choose, ranging from increasing brand awareness to encouraging people to download your application. You will want to choose the objective that best fits with the goal you have in mind for your advertisement.

After you have chosen your objective you will be asked to name the campaign. This name will only be visible by you or anyone else with access to your Ads Manager (so, anyone else that you have given advertising permissions to on your page.) You can also choose to create a "split test" which essentially means that you will create two completely different campaigns and promote them to see which campaign gets the best response. This can be a great way to determine what your audience responds to best so that you can refine your budget and marketing in the future to get the best responses. You can also choose to optimize your budget to ensure that your advertisement is delivered in the most optimal method possible.

Ad Manager

This is accessed by going to your Ads Manager, which can be located in the "Ad Center" section of your Facebook page, scrolling to the bottom and tapping "Create Ad" at the bottom of your screen.

Creating An Ad

With the objective and name in place, it is time to start building your advertisement. This section allows you to outline your objective, offer, audience, placement, budget, and schedule. First, you will want to choose what your offer is and what you want most from the advertisement. The offer itself will be optional but does create a save feature on the ad so that viewers can save your advertisement and view it at a later date. You will be able to pick who your audience is (which should be the exact information you see in your page analytics,) choose where the ad will be placed on Facebook (choose "Automatic" if you do not know,) and then determine how much you want to spend and how long you want the advertisement to run for. Make sure that when you are choosing your budget you select the proper choice from the drop down menu.

The last thing that you will need to do before confirming your advertisement is to create the visual aspect of it. Here, you can choose what page you are advertising for, choose how you would like the ad to look, include any pictures and links or wording, and otherwise design the decorative visual aspects of your advertisement. Facebook now offers carousel, single image, single video, slideshow, and collection style formats. Each of these formats provides you with a different way to share images or videos with your audience. Make sure to pick the one that looks best based on what you are sharing. For example, if you have only one single image, do not pick the "carousel" look, as you will not have enough unique and high-quality images to fill each slot on the carousel!

Following the completion of all of the aforementioned aspects of your paid advertisement, you can tap "Confirm." You will then be asked to confirm the ad one more time, letting you confirm that all of the details in the advertisement are correct and that you are happy with the final outcome. Facebook will then review your ad and, as long as it meets their standards, approve it within 24 hours of you creating it. It will then begin circulating and reaching your audience to maximize your outreach and help you earn greater sales, exposure, or whichever other goal you aimed for!

Boosted Posts on Your Page

Another form of advertisement that you can create with Facebook is known as a "boosted post." This promotion is created by simply tapping the "boost post" button at the bottom of any post on your page. Then, rather than having you create a paid advertisement with specific objectives and parameters, you can simply input your desired audience and boost the post to be seen by more people. This can be a great way to increase exposure and use your already-well-received posts as a way to create even more momentum in your business. Facebook will often recommend which ones to boost based on how other similar pages' boosted posts have performed and the amount of organic reach the post has already received.

Chapter 9: Who is Twitter For?

Twitter is a platform that is used mostly by those between the ages of 18-55. It is really popular amongst those who are interested in the news such as politics or current events, though you often see younger users on there as a way to stay up to date with their favorite brands and idols. Using Twitter is a great way to access a large market, though it does have a learning curve involved that may be more challenging than other platforms. That being said, this book is the perfect place to go to master Twitter, so if you want to take advantage of this platform you are in the right place!

Like Facebook, Twitter has a healthily dispersed platform that ranges in age, demographic, and interests. This means that virtually everyone can benefit from Twitter. Another great aspect of Twitter is that you can see what everyone is saying about you by simply typing your name in the search bar at the top of the application or webpage. As a result, you can easily engage with everyone who even mentions your brand's name, maximizing your exposure in an extremely simple way.

There are many ways that you can use Twitter to market your business. In this chapter, we are going to discuss seven unique ways that you can use organic marketing on Twitter.

These ways will support you in understanding how to get involved in the platform, as well as how to optimize it for your business going into 2019.

Creating and Optimizing Your Twitter Profile

The first thing you need to do to get active on Twitter is to have a Twitter account. If you already have one, this section will help you optimize your profile for 2019. If you do not, this section will help you create a brand new optimized profile that will help you take advantage of Twitter for 2019.

Create Your Profile

The next part of your page that you need to create is your profile photo. Your profile photo will be seen next to every Tweet, Retweet, comment, and other interaction you make on Twitter. For this reason, choosing something that is easy to identify is important. Ideally, your logo would be a great choice as it will help your audience recognize your logo and thus it supports your brand in becoming more easily recognized. Alternatively, you can choose a clear and focused headshot, or any other clear and clean image that represents your company well.

The bio on your page supports a 160 character bio that will help you introduce who you are, what you are doing, and why people should check out your link or follow your page. It is important that you keep your bio both informative and personalized. You do not want to use something generic like "Cheese factory located in Idaho, USA." Instead, you would want to use something like "The cheesiest cheese factory in the eastern states, located in Idaho, USA!" Using something quirky and informative will ensure that your followers know exactly who you are and what they are looking at, but also that they are engaged, interested, and already beginning to understand your brand's personality.

Pick A Header Image

Twitter users are able to put a header image at the top of their profiles that personalizes the account even more. This is also a prime marketing space for giving a great image that markets your best products or services. Photographs of events you have hosted, products, or of your employees all standing together are great for this space. You can also use an application like Canva to create a professional and clean-looking graphic image with text that would allow you to share your motto or slogan, or otherwise, share an important piece of bite-sized information with your followers. Ideally, you should change this image from time to time to keep it fresh and new for your audience.

Relevant Content

Not everything on your page should be filled with Retweets and live conversation between you and other users. You are going to want to post organic, authentic content at least a few times per day on your page. Doing so means that you need to create your own post and share it with your audience. You can do so by tapping "Tweet" and writing a status update or sharing a picture, video, or link with your audience. Ideally, you should mix up what exactly you are sharing on a daily basis to avoid being seen as bland or repetitive in both what you are saying and the way you are saying it.

Your posts should be relevant, interesting, and entertaining in some form or another. Educating your audience, sharing something that will make them laugh or feel inspired, or simply showing off a new product in use is a great way to share. As mentioned in chapter 13, however, this is where many businesses can run into problems. Overly promoting yourself, sharing too many sales pitches, or trying to make hard sales on Twitter through this method will actually take away from your viewers' experience and thus minimize your exposure. People will not like or Retweet your content, meaning it will not be seen. If you want maximum exposure you should focus on keeping 80% of your weekly content engaging, interesting, entertaining, inspiring, or otherwise non-marketing related. The other 20% can be focused on marketing, but should always be done in a suggestive or polite way and not in a hard sales pitch way. In other words "What a heat wave! We have great products to protect your skin during the summer heat – check them out!" or "OMG I love the smell of our new sunscreen – pineapple is BLISS!" is effective, but "Sunscreen on sale for $13.99!" is not.

How to Pin A Tweet

On Twitter, you can have one Tweet that is pinned at the top of your timeline. This is the first Tweet that your viewers will see upon landing on your page, so make sure that it is something important and useful to pay attention to. This could be anything from your latest offer to the most recent news you have available about your company. Once you have published a standard Tweet, simply tap "Pin to your profile page" on the Tweet itself from the "More" option and it will be pinned. You can change this pinned Tweet any time your latest offer or current events change so that your audience can easily see what the latest news is for your business. Once you have pinned your Tweet, you have successfully created an optimized profile for Twitter!

Verified Pages

In 2019, a lot of fake or non-serious businesses will arise to attempt to make a quick buck. This is a growing trend that has been happening for a couple of years now and it is expected to get even worse in 2019. What happens is companies come out of the woodwork, buy a large amount of cheap stock off of wholesale markets, and sell them for inexpensive online. These companies are generally selling poor quality products and rarely have a customer service team to resolve any complaints which are made by their audience. It does not take long for them to accrue a large amount of negative complaints and then essentially fall off the scene. For those who feel this is the way to go, all the power to them. However, if you want a sustainable long-term business, customer service and quality need to be at the top of your list of priorities.

To ensure that your audience recognizes that you are serious about the services and products you offer and that you are focused on quality and customer service, getting your page verified is important. This can set you aside from others by proving that you are serious about what you do and that you are willing to put in the extra work to prove it by having your account verified. To a potential customer, this can be the difference between going to your link to see what products or services you offer, or clicking away for fear of getting sucked into another pop-up business that will be gone in a few months.

To get a verification mark on your account, you need to fill out some forms for Twitter and submit them. These forms will allow Twitter to ensure that you are a real person who is really in business, or who is really who they say they are, and that you have the best interest of Twitter users in mind. You can find the forms by going to Twitter's website, heading into your account settings, and tapping "Request to verify an account." Here, you will need to let Twitter know why you want your account verified, who you are and what you represent, and what your mission is. They also want to know if you have any other websites or social media accounts as this gives Twitter a way to prove your claims against your existing online presence to make sure that you are who you say you are and that they are making a good judgment call in verifying your account.

Video Marketing For Twitter

Video marketing was once challenging to do on Twitter, but more recently they have begun optimizing the platform to be inclusive of video marketing strategies. On these videos, you can include anything that you would in any other form of video marketing films. You can share information, entertainment product demonstrations, educational content, or otherwise to engage your audience and interest them. You can also go live on Twitter, sharing real-time information or demonstrations, or even engaging in a live Q&A call with your audience so that you can answer any questions that they may have and speak with them directly. As with other social media platforms, this form of live interaction with your audience is a great way to show them that you care and to put a face directly on your company.

If you have a company that features many different employees, you might consider giving trusted employees access to the Twitter account using Twitter teams (explained later in this chapter,) so that they can also share live video footage of the goings on in your company. This can be a great way to introduce the many different faces of your team and support your audience in feeling a greater relationship with your brand. It provides a unique and personalized conversation that has been lost in the online space but is rapidly growing in popularity once again.

Taking Advantage of Twitter Teams

If you run a business with employees, or even if you are a one-person company with a virtual assistant, creating Twitter teams can be a great way to ensure that you do not have to single-handedly manage your Twitter account for your business. In companies with a larger number of employees, having Twitter teams can be a great way to get everyone involved, to manage customer service inquiries that come in through Twitter, and to do "Twitter takeovers" where one employee hops on and Tweets for a while before another team member takes over, later on, to begin sharing. This creates a powerful dynamic for your account, giving viewers more to look forward to and helping them create rich relationships with the various members of your team.

Conversations on Twitter

Twitter is all about conversation. If you want to market your business, you need to learn to do so in a way that gets you involved in the conversation. The best way to do this is to go to the main Twitter feed and begin looking at trending topics. Then, you can see which ones are relevant to the general public, as well as which ones are relevant to your unique industry. Once you have, you can read over the conversations and find ways to include yourself. General inclusion, as well as including yourself in a way that allows you to market your products or services are both great ways to get involved.

When conversing with others, you can use two different ways to do so: the first one is to comment on their post. This is a simple comment that is made under their post and that is viewable by all. Or, you can Retweet. Retweeting is like sharing their post and allows you to include a few words about how you feel about what has been said. Either way is a great method for getting involved and sharing in the conversation.

Post Schedule

Posting regularly is important. For Twitter, you should likely have a post schedule that reminds you when you need to post and how often. Applications like Buffer and Hootsuite are a great way to create Tweets in advance and share them to your profile. That being said, you will also need to personally log on and engage with others through your account as well. Each day new trends and conversation topics are arising and you simply cannot predict all of them and account for them in advance through these post schedulers. Nothing will compare to actually actively joining in the live conversation on a daily basis so that you can create updated Tweets that match the daily trends.

So, if you want to have a post schedule the best way to do it would be to have about three schedule posts that go out each day that you can schedule in advance. These should be conversation-focused but not overly focused on trends as the trends you schedule to talk about may be outdated by the time your post comes out. These more general posts should still be informative and engaging, but should also be created in a way where they can add to the daily conversation in general.

Then, you should log in each day and personally engage in the daily trends, even if just for a few minutes. This will ensure that your account stays rich with activity that is both fulfilling and on-trend. That ensures that your account stays relevant, that your audience always has stuff to read about your business, and that you are not losing relevancy by talking about outdated trends or missing out on trends altogether.

Chapter 10: YouTube For Your Brand

YouTube is great because it caters to 59% of the popular who prefers watching video versus reading, and more than 3.25 billion hours of video are watched through YouTube on a monthly basis. The average viewer is between 18-49 years old, making this the perfect platform for marketers catering to a variety of different demographics.

The key with YouTube is understanding that just because you are on YouTube does not necessarily mean that you need to focus on expanding your YouTube following and subscribers. YouTube is a unique platform where you can focus specifically on developing your fanbase on YouTube itself, or you can use it as a unique tool in creating video marketing content for other platforms, such as Facebook and Twitter.

YouTube offers many unique assets to brands in a way that can seriously enhance credibility, interest, and authority. For example, having someone send you a video testimonial of your brand and uploading it to your YouTube account and then sharing it with your fans is a great way to share a more heartfelt explanation as to why your existing customers love your business so much. Alternatively, you can use YouTube as a way to share introductions to your business, products, and services and show your audience why *you* love your company so much, thus giving them a greater reason to love it more as well.

Establishing authority through YouTube can be done by creating powerful clips of you sharing valuable information about your industry. For example, say you run a photography company. You could use YouTube as a way to provide tips on how professional photographers can take better images, how they can edit better, and which software and programs are the best to use when it comes to editing their images. You can also provide the everyday person information and tips on how to take better images with their cell phones, better selfies, and other handy layman tips. Creating a page filled with advice, information, tips, and support is a great way to show that you know what you are doing and that you are happy to help others do just as well.

When it comes to YouTube, you can have your audience engage with you and stay connected with you directly through YouTube by having them subscribe and follow your content directly on YouTube, or you can have them find you elsewhere online. This means that YouTube is extremely supportive in building a native audience as well as building your audience elsewhere.

In essence, virtually everyone should be using video marketing as a strategy in 2019. That being said, incorporating YouTube is a great way to make sure that you are getting the most out of video marketing opportunities since the entire platform is dedicated to video itself. This means that you get the best support, opportunities, features, and algorithms to support you in being found. Furthermore, YouTube offers opportunities for you to make money through advertisements, thus increasing your exposure *and* earning you a small income through the app itself. With that being said, it is a great social media platform for virtually every business to get on. With the right creativity and focus, YouTube could be one of your best marketing tools to date.

2019 will inevitably be the year of video marketing, making YouTube extremely relevant in the coming year. Beyond catering to the marketing strategy of choice for 2019, however, YouTube offers many incredible values to your business, with the biggest one being that the entire platform is built around creating a channel filled with videos. In the modern world, this is akin to having your own television network on cable TV.

Having a YouTube channel that is populated with informative, educational, interesting, or entertaining videos is a great way to create content for your audience to consume. This particular content gives you the unique opportunity to represent your personality, voice, and brand in a way that static images and status updates do not offer. You can also organize your channel effectively to create an entire viewing experience for your audience. If done right, as your page accumulates more videos for people to watch, you will likely find interested audience members binge-watching your content simply because they like your personality and what you are sharing. This is about the most personalized and customized your sharing can get, making your YouTube channel a highly valuable tool for your business.

Statistically speaking, YouTube has more than 1.5 billion active monthly users that collectively watch more than 5 billion videos per day. This is a massive audience to be catering to! If you upload your videos on a regular basis, cater directly to your demographic, and use your account properly, YouTube can be a major native and integrated marketing tool for you to use. Ultimately, getting on YouTube in one way or another is a no-brainer for anyone looking to brand themselves or their businesses.

One last benefit of YouTube is that your channel can earn you greater exposure, and it can also earn you a greater income. Having a Google AdWords account allows you to monetize your videos, meaning that YouTube pays you for these advertisements. While the income you can earn from this is not extremely large, it is enough that it adds a nice passive income stream as you expand your page and increase your exposure. This makes YouTube both a direct source of passive income, and a marketing tool to increase income within your own business.

How to Organize Your Profile

The first and foremost thing you need to do with your YouTube account is brand it. Branded accounts are far more likely to be easily identified by potential subscribers. Furthermore, an attractive branded account encourages people to stay around and browse. On the other hand, a messy one or a seemingly incognito one can result in people growing bored and moving on to the next account that is more aesthetically appealing.

To brand your profile, you will need to pay attention to and adjust six things. These include your profile picture, your channel art, your channel description, your 'about me' page, your introduction video, and the thumbnails that you use for your account. When these are branded, your account both looks great and it caters to your audience in a powerful way.

Your profile picture should once again be either your logo or a clean headshot of you. This makes it easy to identify and is really simple. If you choose a headshot, make sure you use great lighting and a clean background that is free of any distractions or harsh colors.

Your channel art can be customized and made on any application like Canva. This allows you to customize your own art to incorporate your brand, logo, and imagery. You need to make sure that any notable features are maintained within the center of your cover art, as your image will be cut down on mobile. It is essential that you optimize this for mobile as this will keep your page looking clean and professional. More than 500-million videos are viewed on mobile every day, so catering to this part of your audience is necessary.

Next, you need to update your description and about page. Your description is a short one or two sentence bio that will be featured directly on the main page of your profile. Your about page is a lot larger and can accommodate for more information. There, you can share information about who you are, what you are sharing, and why you are the best person to follow for the information or content that you are sharing on your channel. You can also include a point of contact so that if anyone wants to get in touch with you, they know how.

Lastly, you want to brand your thumbnails on your videos. Having a template you use on every single video will make it easier for people to identify your videos when they are browsing. Make sure you use the same template on every single video and that any images you upload into the template are high-quality and descriptive. This will ensure that your videos are both easy to identify and attractive to encourage more views.

Stick to Your Niche

One big mistake some personal brands will make on YouTube is venturing away from their niche to produce content. The idea of making a fun video that is outside of your niche and it potentially going viral is great, but doing so can actually distract from the purpose of your page. It also takes away from your professionalism. Make sure that all of your videos are on-brand, catering to your demographic, and focused on your niche.

If you want to change things up ever so often to add more diversity to your channel, consider instead making different styles of video that you upload. For example, maybe you have two minutes of "bite-sized" videos that offer quick inspiration, information, or entertainment for your audience. You can also have longer 10-15 minute videos where you share more, go into greater depth on bigger topics, or simply pack more entertainment into the video. When you create these different styles of video, pay attention to how your audience responds. The styles they respond best to should be emulated, maybe even turning into a standard style that you incorporate into your weekly strategy.

When you are playing with new styles, it is important that you still stay on topic and that each video continues to be packed with great information. Undermining the quality of your video by over-explaining unimportant topics, being vague or repetitive, or otherwise not packing in great value will result in people not watching as long. Too many videos like this can damage the quality of your overall channel and take away from your reputation. As a result, you may find yourself being unfollowed or struggling to gain followers in the first place. Keep your videos packed with juicy content that genuinely serves your audience and make sure that every video is full of high-quality information or entertainment.

Market Your Videos and YouTube Channel

YouTube channels really flourish when you take the time to actually market your videos. Unlike Facebook which automatically shows it to your audience on the feed, they regularly scroll or Instagram shows it when one of the hashtags you used is searched, YouTube only gives a notification to your subscribers that your video was viewed. Simple notifications are the most likely to be ignored, making it unlikely that your video will reach a high organic viewership rating if you do not take the action to get it out there.

A great way to market your YouTube channel includes sharing your finished video to your other social media accounts and including it in your email marketing list. You can also encourage your followers to share the video, helping it get out there even more and reach an even larger number of people.

If you have a website or a blog, you can also include your latest videos there. Doing a quick blog update about your latest video or having the film embedded somewhere on your website is a great way to have it viewed by others, thus bringing them over to your channel. You can also include a little YouTube icon on your website itself, showing your website visitors that you are on YouTube and encouraging them to hop over to your YouTube page to begin checking out your video content.

You can also post your video on Q&A sites if you find anywhere your video would be relevant. For example, say you find a forum where people are talking about event planning. If someone has a question and you have a video that perfectly answers that question, you can include a short written answer with a link to your video that explains it better. This would then encourage the individual asking to go over to your YouTube, as well as anyone else who may have a similar question or curiosity. This is not only a great marketing technique, but it also drives up SEO as the more your video's link is shared, the more popular the video itself becomes and therefore the more search engines will bump it up the list so that it can be seen by others with similar searches.

Collaborating with other YouTubers is another great way to market your channel. This way, you can share each other's audiences by marketing the video to each of your audience's respectively. This means that they gain access to your audience and you gain access to theirs, thus supporting you in increasing your viewership and vice versa.

Lastly, it is always important to engage with viewers on *social* media. Just like you would on any other platform, make sure to comment back to those who take the time out to comment on your videos. This will ensure that they see that you care and that you are listening to what they have to say. It will also increase engagement rating on your video, thus driving it up the ranking list even more. Furthermore, engaging back with your audience gives you the opportunity to get to know them better and have a greater idea of what they are interested in and what videos they prefer. Then, you can easily begin creating more content that they are likely to enjoy, thus allowing you to optimize your entire YouTube strategy for your viewer specifically.

YouTube Analytics

YouTube will provide you with great analytics on all of your videos. These analytics tell you about important information such as audience retention, watch time, traffic sources, demographics, and engagement reports. These analytics will support you in understanding what type of content is the most popular for your particular audience, who is watching it, and for how long. With this information, you can create a video campaign aligned with your most popular content, targeted at your unique demographic, and customized to the perfect length to ensure that your viewers actually watch the video all the way through. As long as you pay attention and measure for these three particular analytics, you can ensure that you have all the information about your audience that you will need to plan the best campaign that will get you the best results.

Advertisements and its types

YouTube offers two different types of advertisements: video discovery ads and in-stream ads. Video discovery ads are shared at the top of the list when viewers browse for content like yours or match your targeted demographic. In-stream ads are displayed within other videos, shown as the ads that occur at the beginning of most YouTube videos or throughout the center of, particularly long ones. Both are powerful at engaging your audience, though in-stream ones are more likely to get viewed because they are pushed to your audience whereas video discovery ads remain at the top of the list and can easily be skipped over.

With video discovery ads, your key point of being able to attract your target demographic and get them to actually watch your film comes from having interesting content that does not feel like an infomercial, and an attractive title that makes them eager to click. For example, promoting a 3-5 minute tutorial video with a call to action during and at the end of the video is a great video to promote here. Paired with a great title, this video will likely gain views. Promoting a 3-5 minute sales pitch, however, will not warrant you any significant results no matter how interesting the title is because most viewers in 2019 are tired of hard sales pitches.

For in-stream ads, you have about 5 seconds to really capture the attention of your audience before they click "skip" or forget about your content altogether once the video they intended to watch starts. If you can catch their attention, however, through interesting commentary and imagery, then you can retain their view and they will likely choose to skip over to your page or complete your call-to-action when prompted.

Your Objective

Deciding how to plan your campaign requires you to determine what exactly you want to gain from your campaign. In other words, what is your objective? You can easily promote a well-created video that you have already done by simply editing in a few slides that include a call to action. Alternatively, you can create a video specifically for this campaign by choosing what your objective is and planning the entire content around that objective.

For example, say your idea is to promote your event planning business for the upcoming wedding season in the summer. You could easily create a fun video displaying a simple DIY wedding project tutorial, then cut to a scene where you say something like "Not interested in doing it yourself? Then leave it to us at Wedding Planners! We know exactly what to do for your special day, saving you the time and hassle. Save your DIY projects for Christmas, hire us instead!" This makes your video both informative and fun, inviting any DIY-interested wedding parties to hop over to your channel and see what other tutorials they can learn from for their own weddings. This means that you get viewed and shared. It also means that for those who are uninterested in doing it themselves but who are interested in hiring someone, they have found an interactive, informative, and supportive wedding planner for their upcoming wedding. This means that you can successfully attract and retain *both* potential audience members, maximizing your own viewership and supporting you in getting far better results from your ads.

Once you know what it is that you are aiming to do, whether it be to gain customers, increase viewers, get people to download your app, or otherwise, you can easily create a fun, informative, and entertaining video that encourages your potential audience to take action. Thus, your marketing strategy is deemed effective and you can successfully convert ad viewers into customers.

Your Advertisement Copy

If you are going to film a fresh video for your advertisement, you need to make sure that it fills all of the same requirements as any other YouTube film would. The film should be in 4k high resolution filming quality with a great background, great lighting, and a clear and natural speaker sharing your company on the film.

You also need to make sure that the first five seconds of your video is extremely interesting, attractive, and catchy. This is how you can make sure that your audience enjoys what they see and remains interested enough to watch the rest of the ad without simply skipping it to see the video they desired to watch in the first place.

If you are unsure as to how you can film a great advertisement film, consider looking up some samples on YouTube. Watch several videos in your niche and take account of what advertisements come up as you watch. This way, you can see exactly which ones catch your attention and which ones you do not care for and are eager to skip. This will give you a good idea of what your audience is feeling when watching videos, also. The ones that draw you in and keep you wanting to watch more are great quality and are ones that you should consider and learn from when making your own. The ones that you want to skip quickly should also be analyzed to understand *why* you wanted to skip so quickly.

Remember that in 2019, everyone wants a personal connection. The standard infomercial style ads, ones that look like bland or over-used television ads, and otherwise impersonal ads are no longer having the same impact on viewers. Video marketing is taking off for two very specific reasons: *personality* and *intimacy*. With video marketing, your audience gets to see and interact with the personality of your brand and get a feel for who you really are. They also get an intimate view of what you do or what you are selling, thus showing them far more than a static picture that lacks any "life." If you can incorporate these into your video marketing strategy, you will be far more likely to retain viewers and receive a positive return on your investment.

Create Your Campaign

The last step for YouTube marketing is actually creating your campaign! For this, you need to first upload the video to your YouTube channel. Then, you need to go to your Google AdWords account (or create one if you do not yet have one) and select the "Campaign" option. There, you can paste the URL to your campaign video.

Once you have done that, you can add a headline and description for your video. This is what is going to show up in search results, so make sure to include keywords and keep it clear and interesting.

Then, you want to choose the objective. This is where Google will send viewers if they choose to click on the ad to follow your call to action. Ideally, this link should coincide with your call to action. So, if you are talking about a specific product, make sure the link takes them to that specific product on your website and not just your website itself. You can also send people to your YouTube channel if you want to get more subscribers or have more views on your other videos.

Next, you need to set your daily budget. This is how much you want to spend each day on advertising your video. Google will give you a recommended daily budget, but you can set a custom one as well. You can also choose to set a maximum cost-per-view (CPV) if you desire. Note that in doing so, you may limit your viewership. The standard CPV is $0.06.

Lastly, you need to choose your target audience. This target should be customized based on the demographics of those who are showing the most engagement and viewership on your channel. This way, you are targeting those who are already proving to be interested in what you have to offer.

The only thing left to do after this is to review your ad terms and approve the advertisement. Google will then check over it to make sure it is appropriate, then it will be shared out on YouTube as your paid ad campaign!

Chapter 11: Tips and Tricks to Social Media Marketing Success in 2019

In today's world, the value of a strong mentor is well-known. As such, an entire industry of hirable mentors have come up and made themselves available for people who are looking to learn more about their chosen industry, increase their confidence, build a better brand, or otherwise practice virtually any area of professional or personal self-development. For this reason, people now have the capacity to hire mentors if they desire. Choosing whether to hire a mentor versus whether to be chosen by one is a personal decision, but there are many things to consider when looking one way or the other. Let's take a look at the differences between the two.

Having a mentor is not just a benefit or a frivolous option, it is a requirement. Mentors give you the time and attention required to flourish. They listen to you, understand your problems and concerns, and support you in discovering solutions. They educate you on what it takes to become the best in your industry. They have been where you are and they know exactly how you can proceed to reach a great level of success. Furthermore, mentors will hold you accountable and keep you focused on achieving your goals. With a mentor, you have someone who recognizes your passion and devotion but also understands what it is like to have fears and doubts. Because they have been where you are, they know exactly what is required to talk you down from ledges, bring you back from doubt and fear, and inspire and encourage you to remember why you began in the first place.

A mentor will not only be a great ally in your professional success, but they will also be a great aid in teaching you the ropes. If you want to emulate the success of the greats, having someone who is a great mentor to you is mandatory. They will push you, give you some new perspective, and help you discover the answers to your questions and concerns. There is truly an endless number of reasons as to why you need to have a mentor in your life. Having one, especially if you want to have personal success in your personal brand, needs to be a high priority for you. As you begin to grow and get serious about your success, having a mentor is high up on your list of things to acquire and achieve. This will require a strategy in and of itself, as well as a degree of devotion that will show any potential mentor that you are coachable and ready to be a strong student.

Hirable mentors are easier to find and work with. They are actively looking for clients, meaning that they are willing to work with virtually anyone who is ready to pay them. This is a great system as it means you do not have to work as hard to be hired. However, it can also mean that your potential mentor is more focused on running a business and not necessarily the most qualified for the job. For that reason, you will need to qualify your mentor before hiring them. Another thing about hirable mentors is that they may or may not be the best at what they do, and they may or may not be actively involved in furthering their education and staying up to date on the relevant trends in their industry. Even though this is technically their job, not all mentors will do the same. There is nothing that actually regulates these mentors, so it will be up to you to make sure that they are qualified enough to actually mentor you. That being said, if you find a great one, getting the opportunity to work with them is significantly easier.

When it comes to getting chosen by a mentor, this particular choice is a great honor. If you are chosen by a great mentor, this means that they have chosen you above many others in your industry. They see potential and greatness in you, meaning their very choice in and of itself is a great vote of confidence toward your ability to become successful. Furthermore, they are doing the service out of the goodness of their heart, which means that they are there for more than just money. As a result, everything they teach you and share with you will be genuine and focused on your best interest. While hired mentors can certainly behave in the same way, there is always the tendency that they will not.

Choosing whether to hire a mentor or get chosen by one will depend on how hard you want to work to find and begin working with your mentor, how much money you have to invest (if you choose to hire one,) and who you resonate the most with. Sometimes, your desired mentor will actually be a professional mentor, meaning you will need budget to work with them anyway.

Your Role Models

The next thing you need to understand is the difference between mentors and role models. The difference is quite significant, yet both are highly required to support you in generating professional and personal success in your life.

The key difference is that mentors are people that work directly with you and support you in creating success. Role models are people who may or may not even realize that you exist, but who inspired you to do your best in life. Typically, they embody the values that you have or are living the lifestyle that you are envisioning for yourself. This inspires you to emulate what they are doing so that you can create your own success in your own life. Having at least one role model is important because this supports you in having someone to look up to and something to aim toward. In essence, it gives a real edge to your dream, showing you in the flesh what it would look like for you to be where you desire to be.

In many cases, your role model and mentor will be one in the same. Being mentored by someone you look up to and whose success is something that you want to emulate in your life is actually one great way to begin qualifying potential mentors to make sure that you get the right one.

Finding mentors is a three-step process. You must first research potential mentors, and then learn more about that mentor, then learn to get in touch with them in a way that earns you their respect. The first step, finding mentors, takes some time and patience.

The best way to find a mentor is to begin looking at your role models and discovering which one you would like to be coached by. In other words, which one do you like the most, who has the most similar life right now to the one that you desire to have? You should also consider who has the professional and personal achievements in their life that are akin to what you desire to create in your own life.

Once you have discovered a few people who you look up to the most, begin considering which one might be best at mentoring you. Pay attention to what they do, how their strategies are apparent in their work, the amount of success they are continuing to build, and how their personal lives look alongside their professional lives. The more you know, the better you will be able to determine if they share enough of your values to make working with that person worth your while.

The key now to finding your best mentor is deciding which of the few you have identified the best for you to work with is. The one that is the most aligned with who and what you desire to be in life, naturally, should be the best choice for you to pursue mentorship.

Qualifying a mentor is important. Above, we discussed many factors that would qualify a mentor for being one that is aligned enough with what you desire to support you in creating success. However, there are other things you need to qualify a mentor to make sure that they are worth your while as well.

Doing your research will support you in qualifying a mentor. You can do your research by first seeing if that person has ever mentored before. Some people may not be interested in mentoring at all, which may be apparent in their past actions or behavior. However, others may be extremely involved in or interested in mentorship.

You should also pay attention closely to how much your mentor is actually like you. If your mentor is too pushy, rather than just pushy enough to encourage you to do better or grow, or if they teach in a way that is too heavy-handed or not challenging enough for you, working with this mentor may not be the best fit.

Next, you need to consider their qualifications. This is especially true if you are planning on hiring a mentor. Far too many people in the industry call themselves mentors but are not nearly qualified enough to help you get anywhere in your own life. This can result in you unintentionally hiring an under or unqualified mentor if you are not careful. Many can be smooth talkers or have a tendency to swindle people into business with them under the idea that they are perfectly suited for the job. Be careful of this. You must always make sure that your mentor has professional qualifications or marks of success that prove that they are capable of teaching you what you desire to learn. You can easily qualify any mentor by seeing their credentials, looking at their professional milestones, and paying attention to their reputation in the online space. Someone who is genuinely qualified will have plenty of references and resources to show you that prove their ability, as well as an established presence that revolves around what they desire to teach you. The same goes for unpaid mentors, as well. If you are going to look for a mentor, make sure the mentor is qualified in what it is that you want to learn. For example, just because you are inspired by someone for their passion of family does not mean that they are going to be a great mentor for you in establishing a stronger brand and building your professional success as a financial advisor. You need someone who is in your industry and who has qualifications in your industry to ensure that they truly are educated in a way that enables them to educate you.

Another thing you should look for in a mentor are references and testimonies. Pay attention to how other people perceive this person. Read through customer reviews, work-related reviews, and even testimonials or statements offered by those who have worked with this individual in the past. Take the time to get to know them and what supports them in making their judgment on this person. If an overwhelming number of people do not like this person or do not respond well to this person, working alongside them may not be the best idea.

Once you have chosen and qualified a mentor, it is time to approach them. This is not a hugely necessary step in paid mentorships as most paid mentors are happily ready to take on anyone who is interested in paying. However, receiving the mentorship of an unpaid situation takes more planning, strategy, and intention. You need to earn the respect and appreciation of the potential mentor. The first thing you need to do is research this particular mentor to get to know more of who they are. The more you know about them, the easier it will be to talk to them as you will know what interests them, what they are passionate about, and what topics they are likely to want to share with you.

After you know what to talk about, contact the potential mentor. Make sure that you also have a reason for why you have chosen to contact them. This can be anything from being referred by a friend to seeing them at an event and wanting to communicate with them about that event. You want to create a reason for why you are reaching out and make it genuine. When they have contacted you back, then you can move on to the next step which is where you need to explain why you are getting in touch with the potential mentor. Make sure you are honest and clear about your reason for contacting them. Nothing will lose their respect faster than lying, being vague, or pretending you are attempting to contact them for any other reason and then spinning it around to attempt to get mentored by them.

If the potential mentor expresses interest in your request or says anything other than "no," you can begin sharing with them what your reasons for wanting a mentorship with them are. You can also let them know what your goals are. Letting them know exactly what it is that you are seeking, what areas you want to get support in, and what you hope to gain from the mentorship lets the potential mentor know what you are expecting. Then, they can determine if they are willing or not.

If the mentor agrees, the last step is to go ahead and set up your schedule to meet with the mentor and work with them. Make sure that you keep a consistent schedule and that you are always on time. Just because the mentor has agreed to work with you does not mean that they will never change their mind. Continue earning and maintaining the respect of your mentor by staying focused, taking action on what they educate you on, showing up for your interviews, and proving that you are actively engaged in the mentorship. They will not want to waste their time on someone who is not serious, so showing that you are serious is necessary. If you are not ready to concentrate and be mentored, consider waiting a bit longer before choosing to begin working with a mentor.

Conclusion

Thank you once again for choosing this book and hope you had a good time reading it.

The main aim of this book was to educate you on the importance of using social media to promote your company and products.

You will see that it is possible for you to increase your reach easily and get more and more people to like you and appreciate your efforts. The key is to do what works best for you and your company. As you read in this book, there are many strategies to pick from and you have to choose the best. Once you do, you have to implement it and promote your products and services. We looked at the 4 main social media platforms that you must master if you wish to turn your brand into a global image.

The next thing that you need to be prepared to do in your personal brand is to deal with negativity. All brands deal with negativity, but in a personal brand, negativity can feel especially harsh. Because you are your own brand, any negativity that floats around about you can feel very personal. This can be challenging to deal with. However, there are right and wrong ways to deal with negativity. It is essential that you deal with it correctly in order to refrain from tarnishing your name and reputation out of an attempt to protect yourself or stand up for yourself against someone who was being harsh or unkind toward you or your brand.

The first thing you need to know when dealing with negativity is that there is a very specific way *not* to deal with it. If dealt with it in the wrong way, negativity can turn into a major scandal or can have a massively damaging impact on your reputation. For example, you may accidentally reinforce someone's negative comment by fighting back or being a bully back to them. To you, you may simply be warding off someone that is mean. To the rest of the internet, it can look immature, unprofessional, and unkind.

It is essential that you never try to correct someone for how they are feeling about you or your content. This can look as though you are trying to control them or otherwise add fuel to the fire. In the end, this generally ends up in some form of fight or harsh criticism that escalates. In these circumstances, your best bet is to ignore or delete the comment.

If the negativity is offered as constructive criticism and not necessarily hate or harsh judgment being thrown about, handling it with a harsh hand can be unfair and unkind. Constructive criticism does not always feel nice to receive, but it is generally given with positive intentions. Recognizing this and taking the time to respond to these comments and thank them for their input is a great way to deal with it. Be careful not to mistake constructive criticism as a judgment or a mean comment because this can result in you attempting to defend yourself and a large fight breaking out over something that was intended to have constructive results. This can be a very embarrassing thing to endure, so avoiding it altogether by being level-headed and rational when reading and responding to feedback is always important.

What you should do whenever negativity comes up on your page is to truly just ignore it. Negativity is inevitable, especially as you grow. People love to share about how much they do not like things, many times, sharing in an extremely unkind manner. Engaging in these types of people or otherwise commenting back will only result in further fighting. Ignoring and deleting these comments is the best way. Instead of wasting your focus on harsh or unkind negativity, focus on those who support you and are cheering you on. They are more worth the focus and will not result in you handling a negative situation the wrong way and tarnishing your own reputation as a result.

You have to keep with the times and adapt to all the new and upcoming technologies. You have to try and beat your competition and surpass them to reach your ultimate goal.

Through knowledge and experience you will see that it is progressively easier for you to advertise and market your company and make the most of your social media presence.

The next step is for you to implement everything that you read in this book and increase your company's reach.